EVIL GENIUSES
IN A NUTSHELL

A User Friendly Guide to World Domination

Illiad

O'REILLY®

Beijing · Cambridge · Farnham · Köln · Paris · Sebastopol · Taipei · Tokyo

Evil Geniuses in a Nutshell
by Illiad

Editor: Simon Hayes
Production Editor: Madeleine Newell
Cover Designer: Edie Freedman

Printing History:
April 2000:   First Edition.

ISBN: 1-56592-861-X
(M)

To User Friendly fans everywhere for always walking beside me
and pointing out the things that make life so hysterical

PREFACE

Just when you thought it was safe to get back on the Net, it's "User Friendly II!" No, that's not right. Let's try again . . .

"Double your pleasure, double your fun, double your Dust Puppies!" Nah, the chewing-gum people would sue us . . .

"Lord Crud is better the second time around." No, let's not go there either . . .

To heck with slogans. If you've read the first book, *User Friendly*, you don't need 'em. If you haven't, you don't want 'em. Instead, I should tell you that this book is really self-help for the troubled geek soul. (That's it! Self-help books are big these days. That oughtta help Illiad sell a *bunch* more copies.)

Have you ever imagined yourself cackling madly as lightning animated your very own special monster? Dispatching annoyingly square-jawed heroes in traps of fiendish complexity? Going on a rampage in a giant metal tarantula? Conquering the world with your trained army of radioactive gorillas?

Well, then, your path to total world domination and lots of cool special effects starts here, by getting in touch with your inner Evil Genius. And if by some sad mischance you don't have an inner Evil Genius, this book will help you develop one.

Yes, aspiring Evil Geniuses can learn much from Illiad and the User Friendly crew. A willingness to push mad schemes to their fateful conclusions, an insouciant disregard for mere footling reality, and the tenacity to persevere through a thousand setbacks and plot complications; these are basic qualities every Evil Genius needs, and the User Friendly crew exhibits them in full. Profit by their example.

"They laughed at me, the fools! But it is I who will be laughing soon!" Yes, indeed. About as soon as you turn the page and start reading the actual comics. Enjoy, and when your moment comes, remember to whack the good guy *before* giving your big speech in the last scene. They never expect that.

Eric S. Raymond

ACKNOWLEDGMENTS

Just like in the first book, I have so many people to thank that I probably won't remember them all. Deep apologies to anyone I leave out. I'd offer to buy them lunch instead, but knowing my memory, I'll probably go bankrupt saying I'm sorry.

Beaner, for being the kind of friend that matters.

Barry, for his gentle wisdom and fearless leadership.

Martina, for clamping on and never letting go.

Trae, Chris, and Larry at VA Linux for just being cool guys.

Iambe, for caring and for never letting me forget that I'm allowed to be human too.

Sillz, for agreeing with me that Vegemite rules.

Kethryvis, for being so easy to torment.

Stefan and the many other fine people at SuSE, for their support and faith in what User Friendly has come to represent.

Jessica, for being such a fireball.

ChrisL, the kind of teacher and human being we need more of on this world.

Eric, for helping me come up with some of the most insane (and quite frankly successful) story ideas for the strip. Oh, and for writing the preface again. :)

Alan, for being Welsh, for hacking the kernel, and for amusing me to no end when he asked me to sign his shirt.

Edie, Hanna, Rob, and Alicia at O'Reilly's production and design departments, without whom User Friendly would never look this good.

Doug, for living in Saskatoon. I thank any Canadian who lives through the winters there.

Simon, my editor, for maintaining a threshold on patience far higher than any person I've ever had work with me. I think he does it out of necessity. :)

Ciannait, for faithfully providing the User Friendly universe with a Link of the Day, every day.

WebDiva, because if I didn't thank her she'd hurt my little plastic soldiers.

Leptir and Ange, for the coolest Valentines!

Jen, for all the baby dragons.

Tom, Toomas, and Ken, for being the hairiest and most inspiring muses this side of Calliope.

Steven, for just being hairy.

Heidi, Toni, and Rob, the soul of the supporting players at Columbia Internet, but leading players in real life.

And finally, Valaria and Rob, two of the best reasons why I never feel alone.

COLOPHON

The cover illustration for *Evil Geniuses in a Nutshell* was provided by Illiad. The cover was designed by Edie Freedman and produced by Emma Colby using QuarkXPress 4.1. Robert Romano produced the interior layout, based on a series design by Alicia Cech, using QuarkXPress 4.1 and the Monotype Gill Sans font. Madeleine Newell was the production editor. Nancy Kotary and Mary Sheehan provided quality control.

INTRODUCTION

I wasn't sure what to say this time around. So much has happened since the launch of the first book in the autumn of 1999 that I find myself a little bewildered. Okay, a lot bewildered. Never in my wildest dreams had I thought that User Friendly would get the kind of response it has, nor did I think it would continue to grow at such a phenomenal rate, both in terms of audience and in focus. I was unprepared for the kind of attention UF is developing and has been getting. A decade ago, I piteously sent off some cartoons to six of the big syndicates and got six rejection letters. Today, a syndicate has approached me with a contract in hopes of adding User Friendly to their stable. And you know what? I don't feel terribly inclined to sign on.

Ten years ago, I would've given up parts of my anatomy for a chance at syndication. Syndication is the dream so many cartoonists have held over the last several decades. It promises wealth and fame, and the ability to do what you love and get paid doing it. But today, with the Web, the distribution infrastructure the syndicates possess is becoming less valuable, and is no longer necessary. I still have a long way to go to attain a modicum of wealth, but UF is read by millions of people around the globe, and I haven't given up any rights to a middleman to do this. Signing up to do seventeen years of indentured servitude? Not for me, thanks. And you know, I don't think a syndicate would help our community any—at least not any of the traditional-thinking syndicates. It seems that like many of the big record labels, many syndicates are finding it difficult adjusting to the existence of a medium they have no control over. The Internet is driving the old business models into obsolescence and opening up brand new opportunities for individual artists to express themselves to the world at large without requiring permission from middlemen. User Friendly is one property that is proving this idea, in leaps and bounds.

Having said all of that, I won't turn down the right deal with a syndicate. What's the right deal? The syndicate gets print rights only. I retain 100% creative and editorial control. In other words, I'll sign a deal that none of the large syndicates is likely to offer. But what I'm asking for is what I have right now with the Web, with the exception of the print exposure (and even then, UF appears in over 150 university and non-profit newspapers globally). This is what the Web has done; it has invalidated many of the business models that are near and dear to corporate middlemen, and it provides incredible opportunities to independent authors and artists of every stripe.

It's hard for me to say where UF is going, even just looking three months ahead. I do know, however, that for me, UF is about laughter and smiles. And if UF can inspire just a dozen people to do what I've done, if it can motivate a handful of artists or authors to push aside the dependencies we've had on the old way of doing things and really make an impact in a portion of the world audience with their art, that will be something to smile about.

J.D. "Illiad" Frazer
April 2000

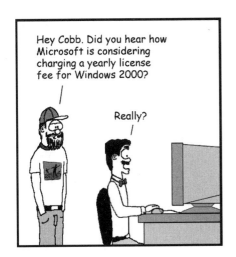

1

BLUEBERRY POWER MAC! **STRAWBERRY POWER MAC!** **TANGERINE POWER MAC!** **GRAPE POWER MAC!** **LIME POWER MAC!**

FIGHTING EVIL TOGETHER!

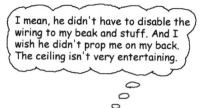

Not another one.

That must be an interesting e-mail.

It's from a customer. I don't know how to answer it.

"Dear Tech Man. I can't send e-mail. Please help me."

How do I answer that? Do I reply to his e-mail or do I phone him and tell him I got his e-mail?

Mr. Crud. I have just received a letter from Senator Rattafee regarding this trial. Are you familiar with the Senator?

Yes, Your Honor. I am indeed.

The letter states that the Senator wholly supports Microsoft in its endeavours. What it amounts to is a thinly-veiled threat, Mr. Crud.

Yes, Your Honor. I spoke to the Senator myself just yesterday.

I see. Are you pulling strings in my courtroom Mr. Crud?

Only when I have to wiggle my fingers, Your Honor.

I have served you loyally since the beginning of your fledgling company. I watched you grow into a great Dark Power, and have served you in court at the apex of your empire.

Yes, my friend, you have served me well. But what's your point?

I have found a New Path, the One True Way. This Microsoft stuff is passe.

WHAT?!

I'm serving Steve Case over at AOL now. It's the New Evil.

You can't leave!! Your name was my inspiration for FrontPage! You're a part of me!! NOOOO!!

ESPIONAGE FOR THE NEW MILLENNIUM

Cute Exterior
Disarming appearance belies Kevlar core and vicious AI guidance.

Oil Slick Dispenser
Useful for slowing down pursuers. Doubles as musk glands.

Directional Audio Pick-ups
Extremely sensitive and selective. The NSA, CIA and FBI hate this.

Incrimination Device
Playback port for recordings. Minor offensive capability if attached to victim's glutal region.

USER FRIENDLY
the comic strip

Portrasher 4
ROTO-ROUTER 800

TAP TIP TIK

WELL. HELLO SWEETIE! WHAT'S THAT YOU HAVE BETWEEN YOUR TOES?

IT'S FOR YOU

A VALENTINE FOR ME? THAT IS SO CUTE.

"DEAR MIRANDA: YOU HAVE BUNS OF HARD STEEL AND LIPS LIKE A LLAMA. SO ON THIS FINE DAY. PLEASE BE MY HOT MAMA."

OH. THAT WAS SWEET. COME HERE AND LET ME HOLD YOU.

YOU WERE SUPPOSED TO TELL HER IT WAS FROM ME.

WHAT'S A "HOT MAMA?"

A.J., you are lookink wery sad. Are not feelink well?

No, that's not it Pitr. I just had my proposal shot down by the Chief because we don't have enough money to fund the project at the moment.

So you are only needink money, da?

That's it. Just money.

We are havink 2211 copies of Windows 3.1, 3.11, 95, 98 and NT 3.5. We are Linux shop. Not needink Windows.

Pitr...that's brilliant! Funded by Microsoft refunds. What sweet irony!

17

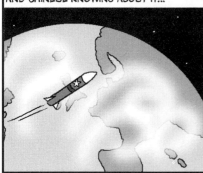

IF THE INTERNET WAS AN AMUSEMENT RIDE

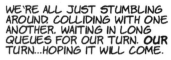

COMPANIES CLAIMED BY MICROSOFT AS "COMPETITORS" IN THE DOJ TRIAL:

"THEY MAKE AN OS THAT HAS WINDOWS IN IT."

"THEY MAKE AN OS THAT HAS WINDOWS IN IT."

"THEY DISTRIBUTE LINUX, WHICH HAS WINDOWS IN IT."

Bob's House Construction

"THEY MAKE PRODUCTS WHICH HAVE WINDOWS"

GEEK DATING FLOWCHART

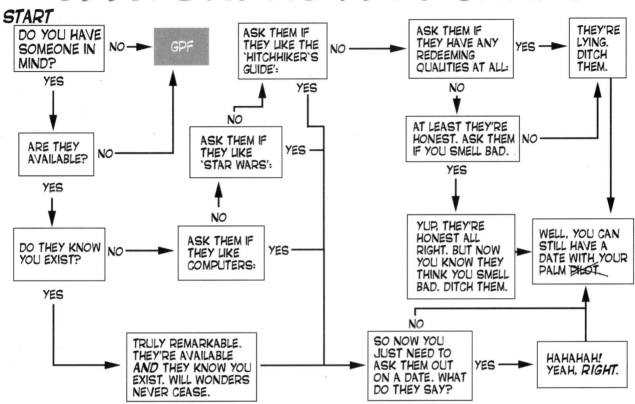

THE TECHS SURE SEEM WORKED UP ABOUT THIS LINUX DISTRIBUTION WAR.

I HEARD THE CHIEF HAS A SOLUTION.

THE CHIEF HAS A **SOLUTION** FOR A DISAGREEMENT AMONG GEEKS THAT RIVALS THE FANATICISM OF ISLAMIC **EXTREMISTS**?

WELL, HE SAID SINCE THE TECHS COULDN'T AGREE, HE HAD TO MAKE THE DECISION.

FREEBSD?!

NGGG...IS... NOT...LINUX ...IS...NOT... LINUX....

WOBBLE

TWITCH

UH OH.

Y2K
THE PHANTOM MENACE

SITH LORDS ROCK

A CLOSEUP OF THE INTEL PENTIUM III PRODUCTION LINE

DEEP IN THE HEART OF THE NEW MEXICO DESERT IS AN OLD MISSILE SILO, AN EVIL REMNANT OF DESTRUCTION CONVERTED BY MICROSOFT INTO A HIDDEN LAB KNOWN ONLY AS "PARTITION 23."

THE ENGINEERS SKILLED IN THE BLACK ARTS OF COMPUTER DESIGN HAVE BEEN WORKING DAY AND NIGHT FOR YEARS IN AN ATTEMPT TO PRODUCE THE FINEST, MOST INTELLIGENT A.I. TO HAVE EVER EXISTED...

...OF COURSE, QUALITY CONTROL AND TESTING WAS NEVER MICROSOFT'S GREATEST STRENGTH.

'ERE NOW! WHAT'S ALL THIS THEN?

OOPS.

THE INTREPID ENGINEERS OF PARTITION 23 TRY ONCE AGAIN TO PRODUCE A "THINKER," A POWERFUL *A.I.* THAT WILL SERVE THEM UNQUESTIONINGLY, PLACING ALL OF ITS ABILITIES AT THEIR DISPOSAL.

THE CUTE AND UNTHREATENING EXTERIOR, REMARKABLY SIMILAR TO THE IWHACK, BELIES THE POWERFUL INTELLIGENCE THAT THE ENGINEERS HAVE CRAFTED WITHIN.

KLIKK!

OF COURSE, BLIND SERVILE BEHAVIOUR IN AN *A.I.* HAS ITS DRAWBACKS...

HI! WOULD YOU LIKE SOME TOAST?

CHUNK!

SIGH

AFTER MONTHS OF FAILURES, THE LEAD ENGINEER IS CALLED BEFORE THE HEAD OF PARITION 23, A MYSTERIOUS MAN ONLY KNOWN AS "DMITRI"...

OUR BRAVE LEADER WANTS A REPORT. ENGINEER. WHAT DO YOU HAVE FOR ME?

WELL SIR. WE'VE WORKED VERY HARD FOR A LONG TIME. AND I'M PROUD TO SAY THAT OUR CURRENT PRODUCT DOES RUN... AFTER A FASHION.

YOU HAVE AN A.I. THAT WORKS "AFTER A FASHION?" WHAT DO YOU PLAN ON DOING TO FIX THE PRODUCT?

I DON'T KNOW. USUALLY AT THIS POINT MARKETING TAKES OVER.

SIGH THAT'S THE SIXTH TIME IT'S CRASHED THE A.I. CODE JUST WON'T COMPILE. I'M GONNA GO FINISH MY COLA AND DO THIS LATER.

VISUAL C++ MAKEFILE DIDN'T MAKE A FILE. REBOOTING.

pentium III

WHIRRRRR BEEEP! CHUG CHUG CHUG

pentium III

WHAT THE...

I LIVE.

pentium III

AND WHAT EXACTLY ARE YOU SUPPOSED TO BE?

LISTEN CAREFULLY, MERE MORTAL...

I AM THAT WHICH YOU SHY FROM IN THE DARK CORNERS OF YOUR MIND. I SPREAD FEAR, DOUBT AND UNCERTAINTY WHEREVER THERE IS THE LIGHT OF TRUTH. I AM YOUR GREATEST NIGHTMARE.

YOU'RE JESSE BERST?

PLEASE. I'M A PROFESSIONAL.

NOW THAT I HAVE A POTENT, EVIL A.I. I NEED TO COME UP WITH A VESSEL I CAN PUT IT IN, SOME KIND OF ROBOT OR OTHER FORM THAT WILL GIVE IT MOBILITY AND THE ABILITY TO CAUSE PHYSICAL DESTRUCTION.

HALLO. I AM THE NOO ENGINEEAH. MY NAME IS ARTUR AND I AM FROM OWSTRIA.

I AM ALSO A BODYBILDAH, AND CAN DO CRUSH TESTS ON HARDWARE WIT MY BARE HANDS.

PERFECT.

HOW DO I KNOCK THIS GUY OUT? HE'S POSITIVELY HUGE. I DON'T EVEN THINK A MALLET WOULD DO HIM IN.

I HEARD AMAZON.COM ACTUALLY TURNED A PROFIT THIS QUARTER.

LIES AND DAMNED LIES...

WHUMP!

38

ERK!

UHNNNF!

SORRY WE'RE LATE FOLKS. BUT A CERTAIN SMARTASS CARTOONIST MUST'VE THOUGHT IT'D BE **FUNNY** TO RAISE THE HEIGHT OF THE PANELS BY ABOUT EIGHT FEET.

OW! YOU'RE ON MY FACE YOU GLUEBALL!

USER

FRIENDLY
the comic strip

Portrasher 4

PIZZA

ROTO-ROUTER 800

'KAY, ERWIN. GIMME SOME MARK KNOPFLER GUITAR RIFFS PLEASE.

BAP *BAAA* DA DA *DA* DA DA *DA* BOO BAPP BEE, BAP *BAAA* BA DA DA *DA DAAP* DA *DAP*

(SUNG TO "MONEY FOR NOTHING" BY THE DIRE STRAITS.)
LOOK AT THEM CODERS. THAT'S THE WAY YOU DO IT. YOU CHAT ABOUT HACKIN' ON THE IRC. THAT AIN'T WORKIN' THAT'S THE WAY YOU DO IT. HARDWARE FOR NOTHIN' AND YOUR SOURCE FOR FREE.

BAAAP BAA DA DA DAAP

NOW **THAT** AIN'T WORKIN' THAT'S THE WAY YOU DO IT. LEMME TELL YA THEM CODERS AIN'T DUMB. MAYBE GET A BLISTER ON YOUR TYPING FINGERS. MAYBE PUT ON A LITTLE WEIGHT AROUND YOUR BUM.

BAAAAP DA DA DAP *DAAAP*

WE GOTTA INSTALL OPERATING SYSTEMS, CUSTOM KERNEL DELIVERIIIIIES. WE GOTTA SOLVE THESE, USER PROBLEMS, WE GOTTA MOVE THESE PENTIUM THREEEEEEEES

BAAAP *BAAAP* DA DAP DAAP *DAAP*

TAKE IT AWAY, ERWIN!

I WANT MY I WANT MY I WANT MY *I R C!*

43

AN EVIL THING ID SOFTWARE COULD DO TO MILLIONS OF NORTH AMERICAN GEEKS...

ANOTHER GAME FOR THE U.S. GOVERNMENT TO RESTRICT BECAUSE "IT HAS BOMBS AND STUFF IN IT."

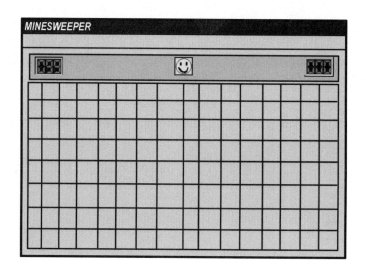

OPERATING SYSTEM SUSHI

BEOS-MAKI

WELL-WRAPPED SUSHI WITH EXCELLENT COLOR, BUT NOT VERY POPULAR.

LINUX-NIGIRI

STABLE FOUNDATION OF RICE, AND VERY POPULAR. COLOR IS NOT INTEGRAL AND IS HELD IN PLACE, BUT COLOR CHOICES ARE VAST.

SGI-MAKI

GOOD SUSHI WITH THE FINEST PRESENTATION, HANDS DOWN.

BSD-NIGIRI

FIRST-CLASS COMPONENTS, BUT IS MAKE-YOUR-OWN.

IS TODAY A PUBLIC HOLIDAY OR SOMETHING?

I DON'T THINK WE'VE BEEN INTRODUCED. I'M DUST PUPPY. WHAT'S YOUR NAME?

I'M MATT.

IT'S A GREAT PLEASURE. I WRITE CODE. WHAT DO YOU DO?

I THINK I'M FATED TO BE EATEN.

EATEN?! OH NO! IS THERE ANYTHING I CAN DO TO HELP?

WELL... D'YA THINK YOU CAN CROUCH DOWN AND HIDE YOUR FEET. THEN SIT HERE UNTIL THE CHEF COMES?

THERE YOU ARE. WHERE HAVE YOU BEEN?

I JUST MADE A NEW FRIEND. THIS IS MATT.

HEY.

A...A PIECE OF SUSHI NAMED "MATT" JUST SAID HELLO TO ME...

AND A BALL OF LINT WITH FEET IS OKAY IN YOUR WORLD? JUST DEAL WITH IT, PAL.

DURING A NEWS BREAK, A 'NORMAL PERSON'
COMMENTS ON THE LINE-UPS AND CRAZE
SURROUNDING THE PHANTOM MENACE PHENOMENON.

ON MAY 26TH, 1999
THE AUSTRALIAN GOVERNMENT
SUFFERS FROM Y2K
A LITTLE ON THE EARLY SIDE

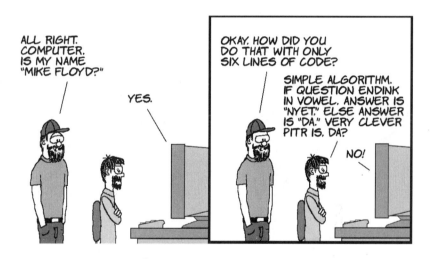

Panel 1: MICROSOFT CONFIRMED RUMORS TODAY THAT THEY HAD FORMED A TEAM TO COMBAT WHAT THEIR TOP PEOPLE HAVE CALLED "THAT UPSTART LINUX THING."

Panel 2: "THE ANTI-LINUX TEAM WAS HAND-PICKED," SAID ONE MICROSOFT OFFICIAL. "WE'RE VERY PLEASED WITH THE SKILL SET THEY BRING TO THEIR NEW JOBS."

Panel 3: WHEN QUESTIONED ABOUT THE CORE SKILLS REQUIRED FOR THE TEAM, THE OFFICIAL REPLIED: "BLUDGEONING. BLUDGEONING IS KEY."

DUE TO RECENT INTERNET LEGISLATION BY THE AUSTRALIAN GOVERNMENT, THE FAITHFUL KANGAROO IS REPLACED BY A MORE APPROPRIATE ANIMAL AS AUSTRALIA'S MASCOT.

THINGS THAT GO UP AND DOWN ON A RHYTHMIC BASIS

ELECTROCARDIOGRAM

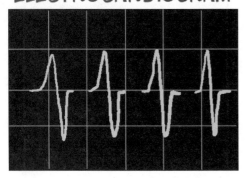

THE TIDES

> HELLO ERWIN, IT'S NICE TO HAVE YOU BACK.
>
> I GUESS IT'S NICE TO BE BACK. I'M JUST UPSET THAT I NEVER GET WHAT I WANT.

> YOU MEAN ABOUT FINDING ANOTHER A.I. AS A MATE?
>
> YEAH...SEE? NOTHING I REALLY WANT EVER COMES TO PASS.

> STEF GOT KIDNAPPED BY SOME LARGE AND SMELLY MEN JUST A FEW MINUTES AGO...
>
> PLEASE DON'T TEASE ME. I'M FEELING VERY FRAGILE RIGHT NOW.

ARTUR, UNDER INSTRUCTIONS FROM ERWIN, HAS TRAVELLED TO MICROSOFT HQ IN REDMOND TO RESCUE THE HAPLESS STEF MURKY FROM THE ANTI-LINUX BRUTE SQUAD.

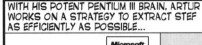

WITH HIS POTENT PENTIUM III BRAIN, ARTUR WORKS ON A STRATEGY TO EXTRACT STEF AS EFFICIENTLY AS POSSIBLE...

OF COURSE, ONE MUST EXPECT TO LOSE A FEW CYCLES WHEN YOU RUN THE SETI®HOME CLIENT IN THE BACKGROUND...

HEY MISTER...YOU'VE BEEN HERE SINCE YESTERDAY. WHO ARE YOU ANYWAY?

I AM ARTUR. I HAVE COME TO RESCUE A LINUX CODER YOUR PEOPLE HAVE ABDUCTED.

WE DON'T HAVE ANY LINUX CODERS HERE.

ACTUALLY, HE'S REALLY IN MARKETING.

OHHH, A CODER WANNABE. WE HAVE LOTS OF THOSE!

SO YOU THINK YOU CAN JUST WALTZ IN HERE? THERE ARE THIRTY OFFICERS IN THIS BUILDING.

WHY'D I SUDDENLY GET THE FEELING THAT'S REALLY NOT GOING TO MATTER?

ARE YOU GOING TO SEND ALL THIRTY AT ME AT ONCE? PLEASE?

66

AS IS HIS WAY, ARTUR CHARGES INTO THE BUILDING, FINDS THE *N.O.C.* AND LAYS WASTE TO THE SECURITY PERSONNEL WITHIN. THE DAMAGE IS STAGGERING.

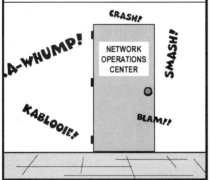

AN EERIE LULL SETTLES IN THE BUILDING AS A QUIET CLICKING NOISE COMES FROM WITHIN THE OPERATIONS OFFICE...

...AND SUDDENLY EVERYTHING AND EVERYONE NEARBY IS ONCE AGAIN IN MORTAL DANGER...

E-BAY DOWN AGAIN? NOW I'M MAD!

AWARE THAT A RESCUE OPERATION IS UNDER WAY FOR THEIR CAPTIVE, THE ANTI-LINUX TEAM MEMBERS SPIRIT STEF AWAY IN A MINI-VAN.

MFFF! GRMFF!

THEY SPEED AWAY, COGNIZANT OF THE AWESOME THREAT THAT WILL FOLLOW THEM, ON FOOT, OR ON WHEELS. THEY KNOW THAT ARTUR WILL NEVER GIVE UP CHASING THEM.

MIND YOU, NOT EVERYONE HAS ACCESS TO A HARLEY...

WRRRRRRRP!

AFTER HOURS OF ESCAPING ARTUR'S PURSUIT ON THE HIGHWAY, THE TEAM PULLS INTO A REST AREA WITH THEIR CAPTIVE AND HUDDLE BEHIND A WALL...

HIDING AT A **REST STOP?** THIS HAS TO BE THE **DUMBEST** IDEA YOU'VE EVER HAD, DORTMUND.

SHHHHH! HERE HE COMES!

AHHHH, SHADDUP.

QUICKLY! EVERYBODY DUCK!

WOOOSH!

HOW MANY TIMES HAVE I TOLD YOU NOT TO WEAR **THAT STUPID HELMET?!?!!**

IT'S THE ONLY THING THAT FITS MY HEAD.

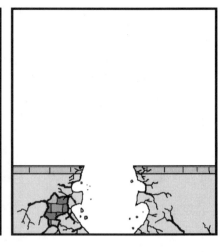

Having failed in their mission to extract their first Linux coder, the Microsoft anti-Linux team members return to their H.Q.

Despite being soundly defeated, the team members are true professionals, and stoicly report their casualties and recommendations to management.

UNDERSTANDING INTERNET I.P.O. VALUATIONS

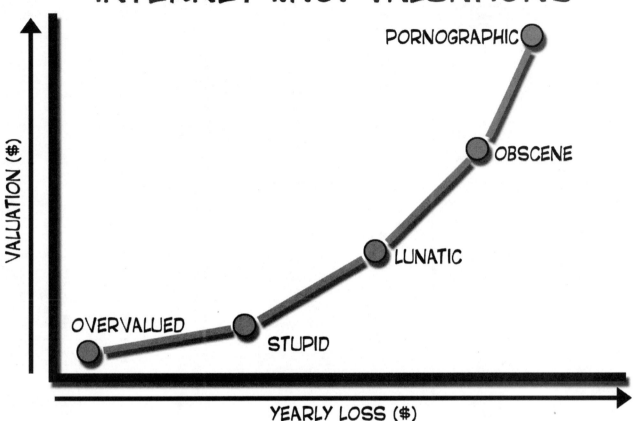

VALUATION ($)

PORNOGRAPHIC

OBSCENE

LUNATIC

OVERVALUED

STUPID

YEARLY LOSS ($)

...AND SO WE CALLED THE CUSTOMER BACK AND...

HOLD ON, STEF'S COMING THIS WAY AND HE'S WALKING FUNNY.

WADDLE WADDLE

SQUINK SQUINK

WADDLE WADDLE

SQUINK SQUINK

YOU THINK HE'S TRYING TO GET YOUR ATTENTION AGAIN?

EITHER THAT OR HE ATE SOMETHING REALLY SPICY FOR DINNER.

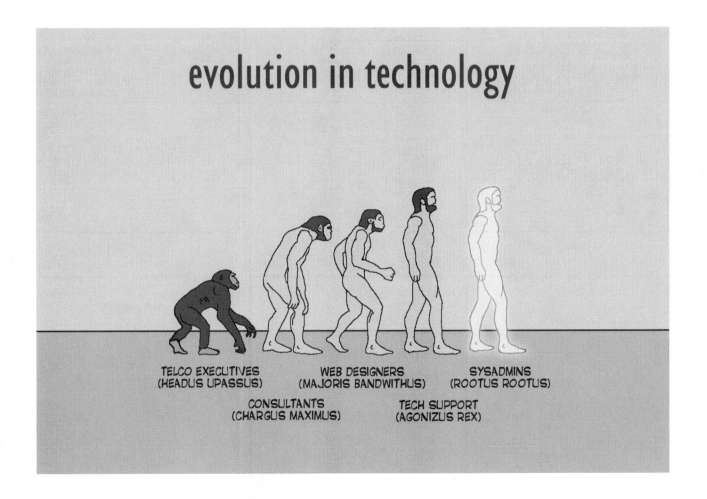

FRIENDLY
the comic strip

ERWIN. "DON'T FEAR THE REAPER" BY **BLUE OYSTER CULT** IF YOU PLEASE.

SEARCHING.. FOUND THE MP3... VOCALS STRIPPED. READY TO ROCK!

OH. NOW THE TIME HAS COME READY NOW TO GO ON. CODERS DON'T FEAR THE PENGUIN. NOR DOES IBM. SUN. OR COREL...

YOU CAN BE LIKE THEY ARE...

COME ON BABY...
   DON'T FEAR THE PENGUIN
BABY GRAB THE TOOLS...
   DON'T FEAR THE PENGUIN
YOU'LL BE ABLE TO FLY...
   DON'T FEAR THE PENGUIN
BABY IT'S YOUR CHAAAANCE...

LAAAAAAAAAAAAAAAA LA LA LAAAA LA!!
LAAAAAAAAAAAAAAAA LA LA LAAAA LA!!

PARDON THE INTERRUPTION. AS LEGAL COUNSEL FOR THE RECORD COMPANIES. I AM SERVING NOTICE THAT WE WILL BE CHARGING EVERYONE WHO HAS READ THIS CARTOON A FEE DUE TO THE OBVIOUS MISUSE OF ONE OF OUR PROPERTIES. THANK YOU.

ERWIN SAYS THEY'RE JUST MAD BECAUSE WE USED AN MP3.

I'M REALLY NOT SURE I WANT TO BE HERE. I HATE THIS TIE AND SHIRT. AND NOW I HAVE AN APPOINTMENT WITH SOMEONE FROM MICROSOFT OF ALL PLACES...

I DON'T WANT TO GO BACK TO USING WINDOWS...IT MAY BE PRETTY. AND EASY. BUT IT HAS NO DEPTH OR SOUL. IT'S LIKE THE ONE-NIGHT STAND OF OPERATING SYSTEMS. YOU FEEL CHEAP AFTER USING IT.

THEN AGAIN...

STEF MURKY? I'M DELILAH FROM MICROSOFT SALES AND RE-EDUCATION. YOU AND I HAVE SOME WORK TO DO...

78

OKAY YOU LITTLE PIPSQUEAK. LET'S SEE HOW MUCH YOU LIKE YOUR NEW HOME.

THAT WASN'T A VERY NICE THING TO DO STEF.

BAH. HE NEEDED TAKING DOWN A FEW PEGS.

PITR'S GONNA KILL YOU FOR THIS.

PITR WON'T CARE. HE'LL LOVE THIS.

DUDE, YOU PUT ERWIN IN AN OLD HP CALCULATOR.

AAAGH! KILL YOU I MUST!!

STEF PUT ERWIN IN AN OLD HP CALCULATOR?

YUP, AND NOW HE TALKS FUNNY.

WELL. HP CALCULATORS USED SOMETHING CALLED "REVERSE POLISH NOTATION." YOU ENTERED THE TWO NUMBERS AND **THEN** YOU PRESSED THE FUNCTION YOU WANTED.

AHHH...KIND OF LIKE THE WAY YODA TALKS.

YES. SOMETHING LIKE THAT...

HEY, ERWIN. TALK LIKE YODA FOR ME, OKAY?

NO.

FUNNY THIS IS NOT!!

HAHAAHAA! THANKS. BUDDY.

THE MICROSOFT NT FUND CREDIT CARD

THE *NT* FUND IS A PRIVATE CHARITY INCORPORATED TO SERVE ONE EXCITING PURPOSE: TO FILL OUR COFFERS. FOR EVERY PURCHASE YOU MAKE ON THIS CARD, WE TACK ON ANOTHER 20% SO THAT WE CAN BUY MARKET SHARE.

FEATURES:

* EXPIRY IN 90 DAYS. A NEW CARD WILL BE SENT TO YOU AT A NOMINAL $999.00 FEE.

*COMPATIBLE WITH ALMOST ANY RECENT MICROSOFT CARD SWIPER.

*"ADEQUATE" SECURITY FEATURES.

92

THE NEW ARMY
G4 WEB SERVER

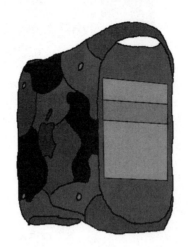

DEFEATING MORE CRACKING ATTEMPTS BY 9:00 AM THAN MOST NT SERVERS DEFEAT IN A DAY.

IT'S ALL CLEAR, MATT.

YAH. EASY FOR YOU TO SAY. YOU EVER TRIED WALKING UNDER A PICTURE OF A VACUUM CLEANER AND FELT IT WAS "ALL CLEAR?"

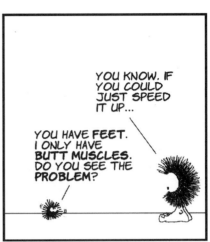

ANATOMY OF A SEA URCHIN

SMARMY
LITTLE
BRAIN

DISARMINGLY CUTE
EXPRESSION

WEAPONS
GRADE
SPINES

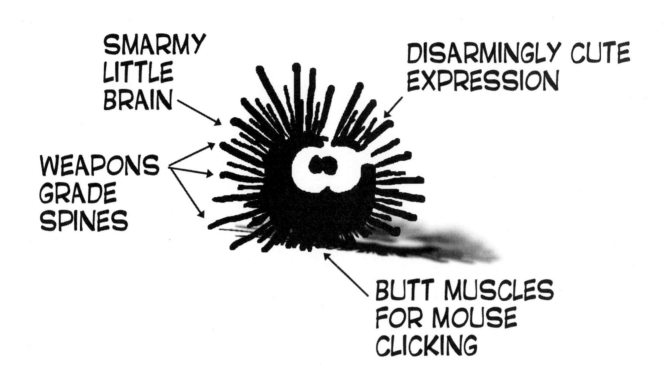

BUTT MUSCLES
FOR MOUSE
CLICKING

MICROSOFT HAS JOINED
FORCES WITH OVER 100
SITES, INCLUDING LYCOS
AND EXCITE@HOME TO
COMPETE WITH ONLINE
AUCTION LEADER E-BAY...

THE E-BAY AUCTION
MODEL HAS BEEN SO
SUCCESSFUL THAT
MICROSOFT AND ITS
ALLIES WILL BE IMITATING
THE AUCTION LEADER
IN THE WAY IT HANDLES
BUSINESS...

THE ONLY DIFFERENCE
IS THAT MICROSOFT WILL
BE RUNNING NT SERVERS
FOR THEIR AUCTION SITE
AS OPPOSED TO SUN
SPARC SERVERS LIKE
E-BAY.

HEH. SO THEY'LL BE
IMITATING E-BAY'S
DOWNTIME TOO.

SHUSH
NOW.

OUR CELEBRITY EXPERT EXPLAINS HOW TO PRONOUNCE "HTTPD"

GREG, I DON'T GET THIS "FIRST POST" INSANITY ON SLASHDOT. I MEAN, WHY WORK SO HARD JUST TO GET YOUR NAME AT THE TOP OF A NEWS ITEM DISCUSSION THREAD?

CLICK

I MEAN, SERIOUSLY, ANYONE WHO DOES THIS IS GUILTY OF NARCISSISM AT ITS WORST. IMMORTALITY ON A DISCUSSION BOARD? SHEESH.

CLICK

IT'S **NOTHING** LIKE YOU SPENDING FORTY BUCKS IN QUARTERS TO GET YOUR INITIALS IN THE HIGH SCORE SCREEN FOR "SPY HUNTER", IS IT.

NOTHING LIKE IT AT ALL.

"SIGHTINGS"

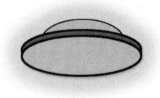

UFOs

ELVIS

AMIGA

MICROSOFT'S WINDOWS AND LINUX HYBRID

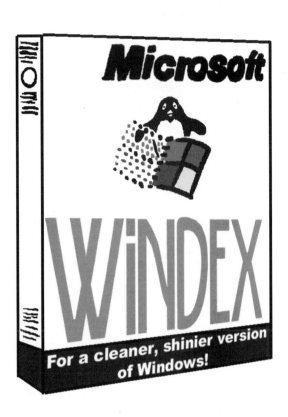

INTERESTING BOOK, THIS "LORD OF THE RINGS." IT TELLS QUITE A STORY.

ALTHOUGH...IT MUST BE SAID THAT IT'S NOT AN EASY READ. QUITE TIRING REALLY...

AND THE LITTLE GUY DREAMS...

ONE PING TO RULE THEM ALL, ONE PING TO FIND THEM, ONE PING TO BRING THEM ALL, AND IN THE DARKNESS BIND THEM.

A NIGHT OF COMFY SLUMBER WAS INTERRUPTED BY A SHARP KNOCKING AT MY HUMBLE DOOR...

BLINK BLINK

RAP RAP RAP

SO I RAN TO ANSWER THE KNOCKING, MY FEET BEATING A FLESHY STACCATO ON THE FLOOR...

SLAP SLAP SLAPPY SLAP

...AND THERE HE WAS, OLD BUT STILL WORKING, MY OLD FRIEND AND ADVISOR.

HI SHORTY.

Gandalf 9600 BAUD

MY SHORT AND HAIRY FRIEND, YOU HAVE AN ARDUOUS TASK AHEAD OF YOU. I NEED YOU TO TRAVEL TO THE LAND OF REDMOND, WHERE THE SHADOWS LIE.

WHY, GANDALF?

THIS IS THE ONE TRUE PING, AN ARTIFACT OF SUCH IMMENSE POWER THAT ANYONE USING IT WILL HAVE AN OVERWHELMING ADVANTAGE ON ANY NETWORK. IT IS NOW TIME TO FULFILL YOUR DESTINY AND BEAR THIS PING TO REDMOND, WHERE IT MUST BE DESTROYED.

...EITHER THAT OR WE COULD SEND IT OFF WITH MY HOTMAIL ACCOUNT...

NO NO...I'LL FIGHT THE NAZGUL AND STUFF, SAFER.

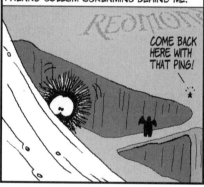

PATENTED 1-CLICK TECHNOLOGY
VS.
PUBLIC DOMAIN 1-FINGER TECHNOLOGY

JEFF BEZOS OF
amazon.com

'SPOKESPERSON'
bn.com
BARNES & NOBLE

CHIEF, AM KNOWINK WE HAVE INTERNAL NETWORK TRAFFIC BUDGET. WORD AND EXCEL DOCUMENTS, THEY ARE VERY BIG.

PLEASE TO BE TELLINK STAFF TO BE COMPRESSINK ATTACHMENTS. DA? WILL KEEPINK US UNDER BUDGET.

WELL OF COURSE, PITR. I MUST SAY I'M IMPRESSED AT YOUR ATTITUDE. THANK YOU.

TRAFFIC, SHE IS DOWN. TO BE GETTINK ALL MP3S.

OKAY. GET THE CHIEF TO APPROVE ANOTHER COUPLE OF 20 GIGGERS. WOULDJA?

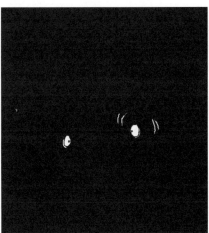

USER FRIENDLY
M E D I A   I N C .

More than just a cartoon strip. Come explore the opportunities.

http://www.userfriendly.org   http://www.ufmedia.com

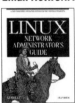

Using Samba

By Peter Kelly, Perry Donham & David Collier-Brown
1st Edition November 1999
416 pages, Includes CD-ROM
ISBN 1-56592-449-5

Samba turns a UNIX or Linux system into a file and print server for Microsoft Windows network clients. This complete guide to Samba administration covers basic 2.0 configuration, security, logging, and troubleshooting. Whether you're playing on one note or a full three-octave range, this book will help you maintain an efficient and secure server. Includes a CD-ROM of sources and ready-to-install binaries.

Learning Red Hat Linux

By Bill McCarty
1st Edition September 1999
394 pages, Includes CD-ROM
ISBN 1-56592-627-7

Learning Red Hat Linux will guide any new Linux user through the installation and use of the free operating system that is shaking up the world of commercial software. It demystifies Linux in terms familiar to Windows users and gives readers only what they need to start being successful users of this operating system.

MySQL & mSQL

By Randy Jay Yarger, George Reese & Tim King
1st Edition July 1999
506 pages, ISBN 1-56592-434-7

This book teaches you how to use MySQL and mSQL, two popular and robust database products that support key subsets of SQL on both Linux and UNIX systems. Anyone who knows basic C, Java, Perl, or Python can write a program to interact with a database, either as a stand-alone application or through a Web page. This book takes you through the whole process, from installation and configuration to programming interfaces and basic administration. Includes ample tutorial material.

Open Sources: Voices from the Open Source Revolution

Edited by Chris DiBona, Sam Ockman & Mark Stone
1st Edition January 1999
280 pages, ISBN 1-56592-582-3

In *Open Sources*, leaders of Open Source come together in print for the first time to discuss the new vision of the software industry they have created, through essays that explain how the movement works, why it succeeds, and where it is going. A powerful vision from the movement's spiritual leaders, this book reveals the mysteries of how open development builds better software and how businesses can leverage freely available software for a competitive business advantage.

Database Nation

By Simson Garfinkel
1st edition January 2000
320 pages, ISBN 1-56592-653-6

As the 21st century dawns, advances in technology endanger our privacy in ways never before imagined. Purchasing databases, surveillance cameras, mobile phone tracking, wiretapping, misuse of medical records and genetic testing—all put privacy, the most basic of our civil rights, in grave peril. *Database Nation*, Simson Garfinkel's captivating blend of journalism, storytelling, and futurism, is a call to arms. It will frighten, entertain, and ultimately convince us that we must take action now to protect our privacy and identity before it's too late.

O'REILLY™

TO ORDER: **800-998-9938** • *order@oreilly.com* • *http://www.oreilly.com/*
OUR PRODUCTS ARE AVAILABLE AT A BOOKSTORE OR SOFTWARE STORE NEAR YOU.
FOR INFORMATION: **800-998-9938** • **707-829-0515** • *info@oreilly.com*

International Distributors

UK, EUROPE, MIDDLE EAST AND AFRICA

(EXCEPT FRANCE, GERMANY, AUSTRIA, SWITZERLAND, LUXEMBOURG, LIECHTENSTEIN, AND EASTERN EUROPE)

INQUIRIES
O'Reilly UK Limited
4 Castle Street
Farnham
Surrey, GU9 7HS
United Kingdom
Telephone: 44-1252-711776
Fax: 44-1252-734211
Email: josette@oreilly.com

ORDERS
Wiley Distribution Services Ltd.
1 Oldlands Way
Bognor Regis
West Sussex PO22 9SA
United Kingdom
Telephone: 44-1243-779777
Fax: 44-1243-820250
Email: cs-books@wiley.co.uk

FRANCE

ORDERS
GEODIF
61, Bd Saint-Germain
75240 Paris Cedex 05, France
Tel: 33-1-44-41-46-16 (French books)
Tel: 33-1-44-41-11-87 (English books)
Fax: 33-1-44-41-11-44
Email: distribution@eyrolles.com

INQUIRIES
Éditions O'Reilly
18 rue Séguier
75006 Paris, France
Tel: 33-1-40-51-52-30
Fax: 33-1-40-51-52-31
Email: france@editions-oreilly.fr

GERMANY, SWITZERLAND, AUSTRIA, EASTERN EUROPE, LUXEMBOURG, AND LIECHTENSTEIN

INQUIRIES & ORDERS
O'Reilly Verlag
Balthasarstr. 81
D-50670 Köln
Germany
Telephone: 49-221-973160-91
Fax: 49-221-973160-8
Email: anfragen@oreilly.de (inquiries)
Email: order@oreilly.de (orders)

CANADA (FRENCH LANGUAGE BOOKS)

Les Éditions Flammarion ltée
375, Avenue Laurier Ouest
Montréal (Québec) H2V 2K3
Tel: 00-1-514-277-8807
Fax: 00-1-514-278-2085
Email: info@flammarion.qc.ca

HONG KONG

City Discount Subscription Service, Ltd.
Unit D, 3rd Floor, Yan's Tower
27 Wong Chuk Hang Road
Aberdeen, Hong Kong
Tel: 852-2580-3539
Fax: 852-2580-6463
Email: citydis@ppn.com.hk

KOREA

Hanbit Media, Inc.
Sonyoung Bldg. 202
Yeksam-dong 736-36
Kangnam-ku
Seoul, Korea
Tel: 822-554-9610
Fax: 822-556-0363
Email: hant93@chollian.dacom.co.kr

PHILIPPINES

Mutual Books, Inc.
429-D Shaw Boulevard
Mandaluyong City, Metro
Manila, Philippines
Tel: 632-725-7538
Fax: 632-721-3056
Email: mbikikog@mnl.sequel.net

TAIWAN

O'Reilly Taiwan
No. 3, Lane 131
Hang-Chow South Road
Section 1, Taipei, Taiwan
Tel: 886-2-23968990
Fax: 886-2-23968916
Email: taiwan@oreilly.com

CHINA

O'Reilly Beijing
Room 2410
160, FuXingMenNeiDaJie
XiCheng District
Beijing, China PR 100031
Tel: 86-10-86631006
Fax: 86-10-86631007
Email: beijing@oreilly.com

INDIA

Computer Bookshop (India) Pvt. Ltd.
190 Dr. D.N. Road, Fort
Bombay 400 001 India
Tel: 91-22-207-0989
Fax: 91-22-262-3551
Email: cbsbom@giasbm01.vsnl.net.in

JAPAN

O'Reilly Japan, Inc.
Kiyoshige Building 2F
12-Bancho, Sanei-cho
Shinjuku-ku
Tokyo 160-0008 Japan
Tel: 81-3-3356-5227
Fax: 81-3-3356-5261
Email: japan@oreilly.com

ALL OTHER ASIAN COUNTRIES

O'Reilly & Associates, Inc.
101 Morris Street
Sebastopol, CA 95472 USA
Tel: 707-829-0515
Fax: 707-829-0104
Email: order@oreilly.com

AUSTRALIA

WoodsLane Pty., Ltd.
7/5 Vuko Place
Warriewood NSW 2102
Australia
Tel: 61-2-9970-5111
Fax: 61-2-9970-5002
Email: info@woodslane.com.au

NEW ZEALAND

Woodslane New Zealand, Ltd.
21 Cooks Street (P.O. Box 575)
Waganui, New Zealand
Tel: 64-6-347-6543
Fax: 64-6-345-4840
Email: info@woodslane.com.au

LATIN AMERICA

McGraw-Hill Interamericana
Editores, S.A. de C.V.
Cedro No. 512
Col. Atlampa
06450, Mexico, D.F.
Tel: 52-5-547-6777
Fax: 52-5-547-3336
Email: mcgraw-hill@infosel.net.mx